W9-ANG-274

D1372748

Structural Wonders

Golden Gate Bridge

Judy Wearing and Tom Riddolls

Weigl Publishers Inc

Published by Weigl Publishers Inc.
350 5th Avenue, Suite 3304, PMB 6G
New York, NY 10118-0069

Website: www.weigl.com

Library of Congress Cataloging-in-Publication Data

Library of Congress Cataloging-in-Publication Data available upon request.
Fax 1-866-44-WEIGL for the attention of the Publishing Records department.

ISBN 978-1-60596-136-1 (hard cover)
ISBN 978-1-60596-137-8 (soft cover)

Printed in China
1 2 3 4 5 6 7 8 9 0 13 12 11 10 09

Photograph Credits
Every reasonable effort has been made to trace ownership and to obtain
permission to reprint copyright material. The publishers would be pleased
to have any errors or omissions brought to their attention so that they may
be corrected in subsequent printings.

Weigl acknowledges Getty Images as its primary image supplier for this title.

Page 24 right: Henrik Sendelbach: page 27 East Bridge; Photo by Rutahsa Adventures,
www.rutahsa.com: page 24 right; Alex Needham: page 27 Xihoumen Bridge.

All of the internet URLs given in the book were valid at the time of publication.
However, due to the dynamic nature of the Internet, some addresses may have
changed, or sites may have ceased to exist since publication. While the author
and publisher regret any inconvenience this may cause readers, no responsibility
for any such changes can be accepted by either the author or the publisher.

Project Coordinators: Heather C. Hudak, Heather Kissock
Design: Terry Paulhus

Contents

What is the Golden Gate Bridge?

Spanning the mouth of San Francisco Bay, the Golden Gate Bridge is one of the United States' best-known landmarks. The bridge was built in the 1930s to connect Marin County to the city of San Franciso. Prior to its construction, people had to take a **ferry** across the bay or travel around the entire edge of it to get from one place to the other. That trip was more than 100 miles (161 kilometers) long. Building the bridge reduced that distance to 1.3 miles (2.1 km), and the trip took far less time.

The Golden Gate Bridge faced many challenges before and during its construction. It was built during the Great Depression, a time when the economy was slow and many people were without work. Even though building the bridge would provide people with jobs, it was difficult to raise the money needed for the project. There were also many people who felt that a bridge could not be built across the bay due to its high winds, strong ocean currents, and almost-constant, heavy fog.

At least one person, however, believed that the bridge could be built. An **engineer** by the name of Joseph Strauss drew a plan to build the bridge and gave it to local authorities. In spite of people's concerns, he was given approval to begin the project. It took more than 10 years to organize the construction of the bridge, but it was built in only four years.

When it opened in 1937, the Golden Gate Bridge was the longest **suspension bridge** in the world. That record stood for 27 years. Today, the bridge is known for its commanding towers, sweeping cables, and colorful orange frame.

Quick Bites
- The Golden Gate Bridge was named for the water it spans across. The mouth of the San Francisco Bay is actually a **strait** called the Golden Gate. Explorer John Charles Frémont gave it this name in 1846. It reminded him of the Golden Horn, a piece of land that forms the harbor of Istanbul in Turkey.
- The Golden Gate Bridge is a toll bridge. It costs money for a vehicle to take the trip across.

Building History

San Francisco Bay was a busy place in the early 20th century. The ferries that crossed the bay were always bustling, and the ports were often crowded with lineups of cars. A local engineer began asking bridge engineers across the United States if it was possible to build a bridge across the open ocean of the Golden Gate. Many said it would be impossible or that it would cost $100 million, which was too much to pay for the project. Bridge engineer Joseph Strauss said it was very possible to build such a bridge and that it would only cost $30 million.

The project began to take shape with the creation of the Golden Gate Bridge and Highway District. Formed in 1928, its goal was to organize the financing, design, and construction of the bridge. The District, along with Joseph Strauss, believed the bridge should be built, but they had to fight to make it happen.

It took workers 30 to 40 minutes each morning to climb up to the site to work.

At first, many organizations were against the idea. The ferry companies did not want a bridge because it would ruin their business. The U.S. Department of War, which owned the land the bridge would join, was concerned that the bridge would interfere with ships coming into the bay. Over time, these hurdles were overcome, and the Department of War gave permission for the bridge to be built on its land.

The Golden Gate uses the longest bridge cables ever made. They could circle the Earth three times.

TIMELINE OF CONSTRUCTION

1928: The Golden Gate Bridge and Highway District is formed.

1929: Joseph Strauss is made chief engineer.

1932: Bonds are issued to fund construction.

1933: Construction begins. The two **anchorages** and the **foundation** for the north tower are completed.

1935: The south tower is finished.

1936: The main cables and steel structure for the road are ready.

1937: The road is added. On May 27th, the Golden Gate Bridge is opened for people to walk across. Vehicles are allowed on the bridge the next day.

1938: Joseph Strauss dies of a heart attack not long after the bridge is complete.

A suspension bridge is a kind of "hanging road."

However, there still was no money for building. Due to the state of the economy at the time, the Golden Gate Bridge and Highway District found it difficult to raise the funds. In 1930, it asked the district's voters for permission to issue $35 million in **bonds**. Voters risked their houses and farms to provide the **collateral** needed for the bonds. They believed that tolls collected from traffic on the bridge would pay back the money. Over time, they were proven right.

Construction of the bridge began in 1933. Factories across the country made 83,000 tons (75,000 tonnes) of steel parts and shipped them to San Francisco. Construction workers accomplished many things no one else in the world had ever done. They built a tower under water in the open ocean and strung gigantic cables 220 feet (67 meters) above the water.

Four years later, on May 27, 1937, the Golden Gate Bridge was finished and opened to traffic. Strauss had built the bridge on time.

Each cable on the Golden Gate Bridge is made up of 61 highly compressed strands.

Due to its unique harp-like design, when the bridge opened in 1937, *The San Francisco Chronicle* referred to it as a "thirty-five million dollar steel harp."

Big Ideas

Although Joseph Strauss is credited as the designer of the Golden Gate Bridge, he received a great deal of help from other bridge engineers and designers. They worked cooperatively to build a bridge that would be grand in appearance but also able to withstand the physical environment in which it would be located.

The first design that Strauss submitted was for a **cantilever**-suspension bridge. When engineer Leon S. Moisseiff and **architect** Irving F. Morrow became involved in the project, it was decided that a suspension bridge would work better and look nicer. With the construction style confirmed, the design of the bridge could be planned. Irving F. Morrow chose to create a bridge that had an Art Deco style. Art Deco is a type of design known for its geometric patterns, bright colors, and elegant, curving surfaces.

The finished product is a symbol of this popular 1920s and 1930s design style. The curves are apparent in the sweeping cables that climb from each end of the bridge to the two rectangular towers. Wide, upright ribbing on each tower's horizontal **struts** gives the bridge texture when sunlight shines on it.

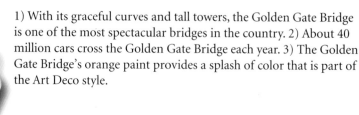

Web Link:
To find out more about suspension bridges , go to www.pbs.org/wgbh/nova/bridge/meetsusp.html.

1) With its graceful curves and tall towers, the Golden Gate Bridge is one of the most spectacular bridges in the country. 2) About 40 million cars cross the Golden Gate Bridge each year. 3) The Golden Gate Bridge's orange paint provides a splash of color that is part of the Art Deco style.

Golden Gate Bridge

Profile:
Joseph Strauss

Joseph Baermann Strauss was born in Cincinnati, Ohio, on January 9, 1870. His mother and father were of German background and had artistic leanings. His father, Raphael Strauss, was a writer and painter, who was known for his paintings of U.S. presidents. His mother was a pianist. Joseph acquired his father's love for the written word and wrote poetry in his spare time. In fact, when he graduated from the University of Cincinnati in 1892, he was the class president and the class poet as well. His main course of study, however, was in commerce and economics.

Strauss' fascination with bridges came as a result of a hospital stay while attending the University of Cincinnati. At 5 feet, 3 inches (1.6 m) tall, Strauss was not a typical size for a football player. Still, he decided to try out for the university's football team. Strauss was injured during the tryouts and was sent to the hospital. From his room, he could see the Cincinnati-Covington Bridge, one of America's first suspension bridges. This bridge inspired him to become a bridge engineer.

Strauss moved to Chicago, Illinois, where he went to work as an **apprentice draftsman** for a local ironworks company. He later joined the engineering firm of Ralph Modjeski, a well-known Polish-American bridge engineer. Strauss worked as Modjeski's principal assistant.

THE WORK OF JOSEPH STRAUSS

Burnside Bridge, Portland, Oregon (1926)
The Burnside Bridge crosses the Willamette River in Portland, Oregon. It is a **bascule drawbridge** designed by Joseph Strauss and built in 1926. Opening and closing the bridge to let boats pass through takes about eight minutes.

Cherry Street Bridge, Toronto, Ontario, Canada (1931)
Strauss's bridge company built the Cherry Street Bridge in Toronto, Ontario, in 1931. It allows Cherry Street to cross over the Toronto ship harbor channel. The north end of the bridge has a 750-ton (680-tonne) **counterweight** that helps lift the center span.

In 1955, a statue of Joseph Strauss was placed on a landing near the bridge in his honor.

While there, Strauss became interested in designing moveable bridges. He invented two types of bridge. One was a type of bascule drawbridge, which uses counterweights to balance the moveable parts. The other was a type of vertical-lift bridge. On this type of bridge, the moveable part is lifted straight up, or vertically, from the rest of the bridge in a flat, or horizontal, position.

With his reputation as an engineer growing, Strauss left Modjeski's firm and formed his own company. Bascule bridges were the company's specialty, and it built 400 of these bridges across North America. However, they were fairly small in size. Joseph had always dreamed of building a big bridge. When he heard about the Golden Gate Bridge project, he saw an opportunity to achieve this goal. He fought for more than 10 years to make the bridge a reality.

The effort it took to build the Golden Gate Bridge tired Joseph. He died in Los Angeles, California, on May 16, 1938, a year after the bridge was completed. A statue of him now stands on the San Francisco side of the bridge.

Jackson Boulevard Bridge, Chicago (1916)

Chicago's Jackson Boulevard Bridge was built in 1916. A bascule bridge, it extends over the south branch of the Chicago River. The bridge is still in use today. About 8,200 vehicles travel across it every day.

Lewis and Clark Bridge, Washington (1930)

The Lewis and Clark Bridge extends across the Columbia River, joining the towns of Longview, Washington and Rainier, Oregon. When it was built, it was the longest cantilever bridge in the United States. Originally called the Longview Bridge, it was renamed the Lewis and Clark Bridge in 1980 after the historic explorers.

The Science Behind
the Building

A bridge must support its own weight as well as the weight of any objects that will travel over it. The materials used to make up the bridge, as well as the design of the bridge, all must work together to create a strong structure. The Golden Gate Bridge is elegant in its look, but it is also very strong. As a result, it is able to withstand high winds and fast-moving waters, as well as hold the traffic that crosses it each day.

The Science of Suspension

Suspension bridges, such as the Golden Gate Bridge, work due to the forces of **compression** and **tension**. These forces are used to support the weight of the bridge and its cargo. They do this by allowing the weight of the bridge and its traffic to be transferred to other points.

The roadway of the Golden Gate Bridge hangs from cables that stretch across the bridge's entire span, running through the bridge's two towers. The towers help to support the roadway's weight. Compression presses down on the roadway, but the cables counter this pressure by pushing it

Fog makes it difficult for incoming ships to see the Golden Gate Bridge. To make it more visible, the U.S. Navy wanted the bridge to be painted black with yellow stripes.

into the towers. From there, the pressure moves down the towers and into the earth. The bridge stays stable as a result.

The forces of tension are handled by the bridge's supporting cables. These cables are attached to the bridge's anchorages. The weight of the bridge, along with the weight of the traffic crossing the bridge, stretch the cables tight, causing tension. This tension is relayed to the anchorages, which, like the towers, are built into the ground. The tension from the cables is directed to the ground, taking the pressure off the bridge itself and keeping it firmly in place.

Trusses

Due to their length and use of cables, suspension bridges are exposed to a force called torsion. This is a twisting force normally caused by high winds. If not controlled, it can seriously damage a bridge. On the Golden Gate Bridge, this force is combatted through the use of trusses. A truss is a type of framework made up of metal or wood that gives a structure **rigidity**. The trusses on the Golden Gate Bridge provide reinforcement to the bridge's **deck**. This makes it more resistant to twisting forces. In recent years, the trusses have been refitted with newer, stronger materials. This helps to keep the bridge from collapsing due to twisting movements during earthquakes.

Web Link:
To find out more about how compression and tension affect bridges, go to http://science.howstuffworks.com/bridge.htm

Science and Technology

Building the Golden Gate Bridge required planning, labor, and the best technology available at the time. Sometimes, technology relies on scientific principles from the past. In the case of the Golden Gate Bridge, the construction machines used were often made up of **simple machines**, such as pulleys and wedges. However, for some of the construction, new methods and machinery were used.

Pulleys

A very large amount of steel had to be moved during the building of the Golden Gate Bridge. Due to the weight of the steel, a crane was used to move the pieces into place. Cranes use pulleys to lift heavy loads easily. Pulleys are wheels with a groove around the edge. Ropes or cables are pulled along the groove to reduce the weight of the load. The more wheels the pulley system has, the more the weight is shared between them.

Rivets

There are more than one million steel rivets holding the Golden Gate Bridge together. A rivet is a short shaft of metal with a rounded head that is narrow at one end and gradually widens at the other end. When two pieces of steel are joined, a hole is drilled through both. The rivet is put through the hole and is then hit with a hammer. The hammer spreads the end of the rivet. This makes one end of the rivet wider, holding the two pieces of metal in place.

The pulleys used to construct the Golden Gate Bridge had many wheels. This made it easier to lift pieces of the bridge that weighed many tons.

The flattened end of a rivet holds the steel pieces firmly together.

It took 80,000 miles (128,748 km) of wire to make the Golden Gate Bridge's main cables.

Spinning the Cable

At the time, no other object had ever been built that was similar to the suspension cables of the Golden Gate Bridge. Each cable is made of small wires that have been bound together very tightly. Great pressure is needed to force thousands of tons of steel wire into a perfect round shape. To do this, the wires were bound around giant spools that were attached to the bridge's anchorages. One end of the wire was tied to part of the anchorage, while the rest of the wire was wound around the giant wheel. This wheel was then pushed across the bridge, with the cable unwinding as the wheel rolled. Once the wheel reached the other side of the bridge, the end of the cable was attached to that side's anchorage, and the process began again. Spinning the cables took a great deal of time. To speed up the process, two wheels were used at the same time. Each started at opposite ends of the bridge and passed by each other in the center.

Quick Bites

- From July to October, foghorns on the bridge can be heard for about five hours each day. They help boats avoid a crash with the towers and the shore.
- There are 600,000 rivets in each tower that hold the steel pieces together. Every one of them was tightened by hand.

Computer-Aided Design

Architects are trained professionals who work with clients to design structures. Before anything is built, they make detailed drawings or models. These plans are important tools that help people visualize what the structure will look like. A blueprint is a detailed diagram that shows where all the parts of the structure will be placed. Walls, doors, windows, plumbing, electrical wiring, and other details are mapped out on the blueprint. Blueprints act as a guide for engineers and builders during construction.

For centuries, architects and builders worked without the aid of computers. Sketches and blueprints were drawn by hand. Highly skilled drafters would draw very technical designs. Today, this process is done using computers and sophisticated software programs. Architects use CAD, or computer-aided design, throughout the design process. Early CAD systems used computers to draft building plans. Today's computer programs can do much more. They can build three-dimensional models and computer simulations of how a building will look. They can also calculate the effects of different physical forces on the structure. Using CAD, today's architects can build more complex structures at lower cost and in less time.

Computer-aided design programs have been used since the 1960s.

Eye on Design

Testing the Old with the New

Today, engineers use highly technical computer programs to make drawings and calculations.

When the Golden Gate Bridge was built, engineers did most of their planning with pencils and paper. Today, engineers can use computer programs to help them plan and figure out complex problems. Computers also can be used to research any questions an engineer might have about bridge construction, such as how much a bridge can sway without breaking, or what can happen to a bridge during an earthquake.

Some companies are hired to study old bridges. They use computer programs to look for weak places on a bridge. All kinds of information about the bridge are put into the computer. Measurements about how the bridge moves in the wind, and the size and strength of its different parts are compiled. In this way, a computer model of the bridge is made. The model is put through a series of tests to see how it will react to certain situations, such as earthquakes and other forces. The computer calculates where the structure might fail.

This kind of testing has been done on the Golden Gate Bridge. Engineers found ways the bridge could be strengthened to help it survive earthquakes. Work is continually being done to correct these problems.

MEASURING THE GOLDEN GATE BRIDGE

Location

The Golden Gate Bridge is located at the mouth of San Francisco Bay, in the state of California, on the west coast of the United States.

NEVADA

San Francisco Bay

Pacific
Ocean

CALIFORNIA

N
W+E
S

Height

- The towers stretch 746 feet (227 m) above the water.
- The deck is 220 feet (67 m) above the water.

Length

- The bridge is 8,981 feet (2,737 m) long in total. The longest span, from the north to south tower, is 4,200 feet (1,280 m) long.
- The bridge's main cables are 7,650 feet (2,332 m) long.

Weight

- Each anchorage weighs 60,000 tons (54,431 tonnes).
- The entire bridge weighs 887,000 tons (804,673 tonnes).

Other Interesting Facts

- On opening day in 1937, 18,000 people lined up at 6:00 a.m. to be the first to cross the bridge. Some even crossed on stilts or walked backwards.
- During construction, a net was strung under the bridge. It saved the lives of 19 workers and is now a standard safety feature in bridge building.

Movement

The Golden Gate Bridge has been designed to sway 27.7 feet (8.4 m) in the event of an earthquake.

Environmental Viewpoint

Tides enter and leave the bay twice a day, crashing against the bridge's underwater supports. Winds whip past the cables and push against the road deck, causing the bridge to sway. The salty sea water and high humidity get under the bridge's paint and cause metal **corrosion**. As a result, the bridge's condition needs to be checked all the time so that any potential problems can be fixed.

In some cases, minor repairs are done on the bridge. The paint is "touched up" in areas where breaks have occurred. Steelworkers replace rivets and steel bars that are badly corroded. Sometimes, however, the bridge needs more serious work done to it. The bridge has undergone many renovations since it was first built. In the 1950s, it was outfitted with a bracing system to improve its stability. In the 1980s, the entire deck was replaced due to salt and humidity damage. This work took years to complete.

In addition to these problems, San Francisco Bay lies in a region where two of the Earth's **tectonic plates** meet. When these plates move against each other, an earthquake can occur. The San Francisco area is under constant threat of earthquakes. When one occurs, the bridge needs to be able to withstand the intense movement. It has already survived one earthquake, in 1989, but concerns remain about the bridge's strength and stability.

Storms sometimes threaten the safety of vehicles driving across the Golden Gate Bridge. However, the bridge has only been closed three times due to high winds.

In 1997, work began to make the Golden Gate Bridge more resistant to earthquakes. Almost every part of the bridge is having repairs or renovations done to it. Foundations and trusses are being strengthened. Supporting towers and braces are being replaced. New parts are being added to the bridge to help it adjust to the extreme shifting an earthquake can cause. The project is taking place in three stages. It is expected to be complete in 2013.

BRIDGE POLLUTION

While the environment has a direct impact on the Golden Gate Bridge, the bridge has also affected its environment. With the high volume of vehicles that cross the bridge everyday comes pollution caused by car exhaust. This exhaust puts dangerous gases into the air. They can cause problems ranging from difficulty in breathing to **acid rain**.

Actions have been taken to reduce this pollution problem. Campaigns have been run that urge people to use city buses instead of their cars to travel across the bridge. This means more people can travel with less exhaust created. Those who do travel in cars are encouraged to carpool. People going to work with two or more passengers in their car do not have to pay the $6 bridge toll.

Construction Careers

The Golden Gate Bridge was built during the Great Depression. This was a time when many people did not have jobs. No one knows how many people worked on the bridge, but they came from all kinds of backgrounds. Farmers and office clerks became steelworkers so that they could help construct the bridge. Cement workers built the anchorages. Engineers planned, designed, and managed the construction process.

Cement Masons

Cement masons specialize in handling cement and concrete. They pour wet concrete into molds and make sure it spreads to the necessary thickness. They then level and smooth the surfaces and edges of the cement. Throughout the process, cement masons check how the wind and temperature are affecting the concrete and fix any potential problems. Working with cement is very physical work. Cement masons often kneel and bend over the surface they are working on. They also carry heavy bags of cement. This requires a great deal of physical strength.

Steelworkers

Steel makes up a good part of the Golden Gate Bridge. Steelworkers put the metal pieces together. They read the engineer's blueprints, and then, put the bridge's framework together. This involved welding or bolting the correct pieces in place. Steelworkers continue to work on the Golden Gate Bridge. They need to be in good physical condition and have good mechanical skills. Steelworkers should be able to use a variety of tools to inspect the bridge parts and replace any that are worn.

Painters

The Golden Gate Bridge painters have to be very comfortable with extreme heights. When painting, they are often suspended high on the bridge. Here, they feel the full brunt of high winds, fog, rain, and other weather conditions while wearing only a small harness to hold them in place. The Golden Gate Bridge needs paint to protect its metal from rusting in the salty sea air, so the role of the painter is very important. The entire bridge has only been repainted three times. Most of the time, painters touch up problem areas. They find spots that are degrading as a result of smog and car exhaust. They quickly remove the damaged paint using hand tools or sandblasters. After cleaning the area, they apply a fresh coat of paint. It takes 38 painters, working year-round, to maintain the paint on the bridge.

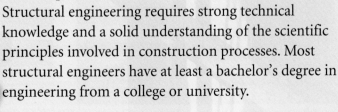

Structural Engineers

Structural engineers make sure structures are built to be safe, strong, and stable. They ensure that the bridge's design and construction materials will survive the pressures of the bridge's environment. In the case of the Golden Gate Bridge, this includes strong water currents, high winds, and potential earthquakes. Structural engineering requires strong technical knowledge and a solid understanding of the scientific principles involved in construction processes. Most structural engineers have at least a bachelor's degree in engineering from a college or university.

Web Link:
To find out more about structural engineering, visit www.pbs.org/wgbh/buildingbig/profile/career/structural.html.

Notable Structures

Suspension bridges have been used for a very long time. Ancient peoples, such as the Incas, built bridges suspended by cables. Over time, these bridges became more complex. They were designed to span longer and wider areas and to hold heavier cargo.

Akashi Kaikyo Bridge

Built: 1998

Location: Kobe and Awaji-shima, Japan

Design: Honshu-Shikoku Bridge Authority

Description: Also known as the Pearl Bridge, the Akashi Kaikyo Bridge is now the longest suspension bridge in the world. It is 12,828 feet (3,910 m) long, with towers that are 928 feet (283 m) tall. This bridge is built to stand up to strong winds, **tsunamis**, and earthquakes.

Inca Suspension Bridge

Built: 16th century to present

Location: Huinchiri, Peru

Design: Incas

Description: Known as the last Inca hanging bridge, this bridge extends across the Apurimac River. It is made from stiff grasses woven into a strong, thick rope that is 150 feet (46 m) long. Villagers from both sides of the river come together for three days every year to make new rope for it. They do this to honor their past.

These bridges often became known for their beauty. With their high towers, gliding cables, and elegant appearance, suspension bridges often become important landmarks for the places where they reside. Some countries have even placed them in national protection programs to preserve them for years to come.

Brooklyn Bridge

Built: 1883

Location: Manhattan and Brooklyn, New York, United States

Design: John Roebling

Description: The Brooklyn Bridge joins Brooklyn to New York City. It spans 1,595 feet (486 m) and is the second-busiest bridge in New York City. During its construction, John Roebling died. His son, Washington, took over the project but became ill. His wife helped him complete the bridge.

Union Bridge

Built: 1820

Location: Horncliffe, United Kingdom

Design: Captain Samuel Brown

Description: One lane of traffic travels 449 feet (137 m) over the River Tweed on the Union Bridge. As the oldest suspension bridge still in use, it is protected as an ancient monument. This means that it is considered to be a structure of national importance and, as a result, cannot be changed in any way without special permission.

Suspension Bridges Around the World

Suspension bridges can be found all over the world. Some are used for car traffic, while others carry pedestrians and trains.

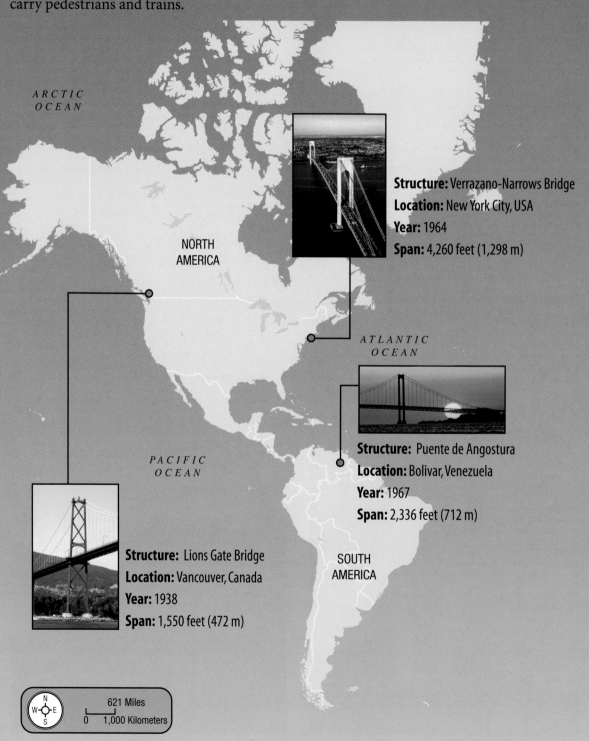

Structure: Verrazano-Narrows Bridge
Location: New York City, USA
Year: 1964
Span: 4,260 feet (1,298 m)

Structure: Puente de Angostura
Location: Bolivar, Venezuela
Year: 1967
Span: 2,336 feet (712 m)

Structure: Lions Gate Bridge
Location: Vancouver, Canada
Year: 1938
Span: 1,550 feet (472 m)

ARCTIC OCEAN

NORTH AMERICA

ATLANTIC OCEAN

PACIFIC OCEAN

SOUTH AMERICA

621 Miles
0   1,000 Kilometers

When there are long distances to cover, suspension bridges are the choice of engineers. This map shows some of the world's better known suspension bridges.

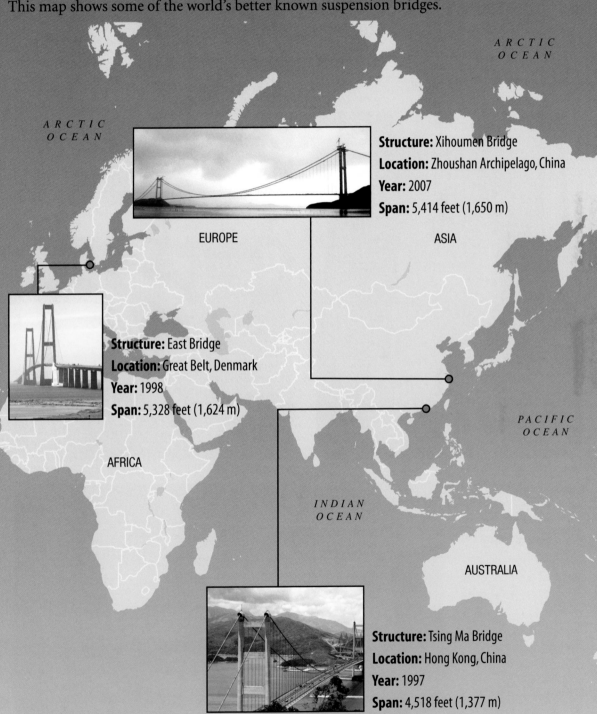

ARCTIC OCEAN

ARCTIC OCEAN

EUROPE

ASIA

Structure: Xihoumen Bridge
Location: Zhoushan Archipelago, China
Year: 2007
Span: 5,414 feet (1,650 m)

Structure: East Bridge
Location: Great Belt, Denmark
Year: 1998
Span: 5,328 feet (1,624 m)

AFRICA

PACIFIC OCEAN

INDIAN OCEAN

AUSTRALIA

Structure: Tsing Ma Bridge
Location: Hong Kong, China
Year: 1997
Span: 4,518 feet (1,377 m)

Quiz

Q Was the Golden Gate the first suspension bridge in the world?

A No. Suspension bridges, in some form, have been around for centuries. Ancient cultures, such as the Incas, were known to have built suspension bridges.

Q What is the name of the Golden Gate Bridge's design style?

A The bridge was designed using the Art Deco style. This was a popular design style in the 1920s.

Q Did Joseph Strauss design the bridge by himself?

A No. Many engineers and designers helped Joseph Strauss plan the Golden Gate Bridge.

Q What are the two main forces suspension bridges rely on?

A Suspension bridges work as a result of the forces of compression and tension. These forces support the weight of the bridge and its traffic by diverting the pressure to other points.

Build a Suspension Bridge

A suspension bridge has five main parts. These are towers, anchorages, main cables, suspending cables, and a deck. Try building a model suspension bridge using materials you may have around the house.

Materials
- six paper towel rolls
- glue
- long pipe cleaners
- scissors
- cardboard pizza box
- toy car
- corrugated cardboard
- pen or pencil

Instructions
1. Cut two of the paper towel rolls in half. The full cardboard rolls will be your bridge's towers, and the half-rolls will be its anchorages.
2. Glue the towers to the center of the pizza box. Then, glue two anchorages to each edge of the box. Let the glue dry.
3. Cut small slits into the tops of the towers and anchorages. To begin making the bridge's cable, make a knot in the end of a pipe cleaner. Put the knotted end into one of the slits. Link other pipe cleaners to the end to make the cable longer. String the pipe cleaners from one set of anchorages to the two sets of towers and then to the other set of anchorages.
4. To make the bridge deck, measure the width and length of the bridge. Draw these measurements onto a piece of corrugated cardboard, and then cut out the shape.
5. To suspend the bridge's deck, take several pipe cleaners and bend their tips around the bridge's main cables. Make sure the pipe cleaners extend along the length of the entire bridge, from anchorage to anchorage. Pass these pipe cleaners under the deck and then attach them to the cables on the other side of the bridge. If you need more length, twist more pipe cleaners together. When complete, adjust the pipe cleaners until the deck hangs parallel to the base.
6. How much weight does your bridge hold? Try running a toy car across it. Does the bridge hold the weight of the car? If not, how could you make your bridge stronger?

Further Research

You can find more information on the Golden Gate Bridge, suspension bridges around the world, or the building of bridges at your local library or on the Internet.

Websites

For more information about the Golden Gate Bridge, visit www.goldengatebridge.org

Learn more about suspension bridges at www.bridgemeister.com

Find out more about how bridges work, visit www.howstuffworks.com/bridge.htm

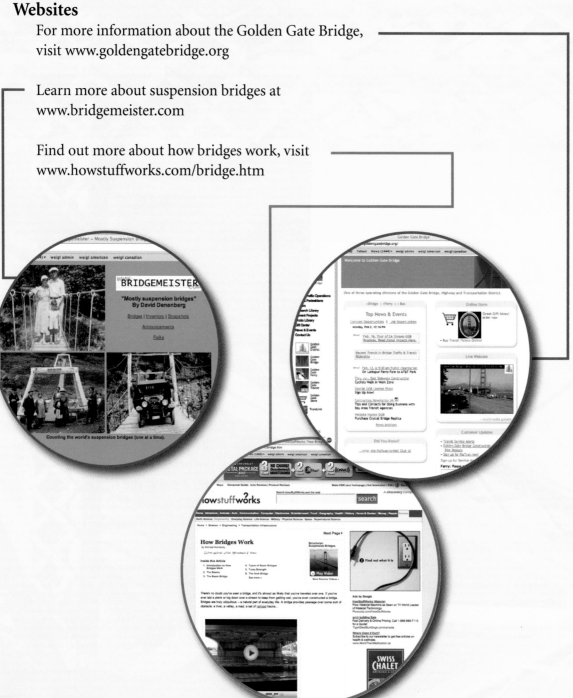

Glossary

acid rain: rain that has been contaminated by air pollution; can damage buildings, harm wildlife, and pollute water supplies

anchorages: structures used to hold something else firmly in place

apprentice: someone who is being trained for a job

architect: someone who designs and supervises the construction of a building or other structure

bascule drawbridge: a bridge that opens to allow boats to pass through; uses a heavy counterweight to help open and close the bridge

bonds: certificates of debt issued in order to raise funds

cantilever: a structural framework that is fixed at one end only

collateral: security pledged for the repayment of a loan

compression: the act of being flattened or squeezed together by pressure

corrosion: a process in which an object is worn away by a chemical action

counterweight: an object that balances opposing forces

deck: a platform on which bridge traffic travels

draftsman: someone who draws or sketches building plans

engineer: someone who applies scientific principles to the design of structures

ferry: a boat used to carry people and vehicles across water

foundation: the part of a structure that helps support its weight

rigidity: stiffness

simple machines: devices that overcome resistance at one point by applying force at some other point

strait: a narrow passage of water that links two larger bodies of water

struts: the bracing pieces of a structure's framework

suspension bridge: a bridge that has a deck supported by cables that are anchored at both ends

tectonic plates: pieces of Earth's surface that are constantly moving

tension: the state of being stretched

tsunamis: high sea waves caused by natural events, such as earthquakes

Index